THE OTHER NOW

First published in 2016 by
The Dedalus Press
13 Moyclare Road
Baldoyle
Dublin D13 K1C2
Ireland

www.**dedaluspress**.com

ISBN 978 1 910251 23 2

Dedalus Press titles are represented in the UK by
Central Books, 99 Wallis Road, London E9 5LN
and in North America by Syracuse University Press, Inc.,
621 Skytop Road, Suite 110, Syracuse, New York 13244

Cover image 'Face 3', oil on canvas, 100 x 100 cm
by Abdel Raouf Al Ajouri
by permission of the artist

The Dedalus Press receives financial assistance from
The Arts Council / An Chomhairle Ealaíon.

THE OTHER NOW
New and Selected Poems

Catherine Ann Cullen

DEDALUS PRESS

To my siblings
Pat, John, Romy, Lisa and Jennifer:
ar scáth a chéile muid.

CONTENTS

❧

The Other Now – New Poems

❧

from *A Bone in My Throat* (2007)

⌒

from *Strange Familiar* (2013)

The Other Now
New Poems

The Other Now

As the guests dispersed
the stairs folded you in their zigzag hold
and your fairy godmother placed two sweets
in your upturned palms.

You pondered their wrappers,
slipped one lozenge into the kangaroo pouch of your dress,
and unwound the other from its foil.
'I'll eat this now,' you said.
'And what will you do with the other?'
Bending your white head to check it, you smiled,
'I'll keep that for the other now.'

Time and again I have flung
a net of words over that moment,
but it is always another now I capture,
never quite catching
the perfect size of you:
small for two, articulate,
hair gleaming like a dawn beach,
eyes combing the world.

And while I collect moments
in paper pockets,
how many have you piled up
like your darkening hair?

Is there one we share
or do I stand apart
sucking your phrases down
to a stain on my tongue
while you sit white on the stair
glossing the future?

The Dark Room

All the coats were haystacked on your bed,
the old shoes huddled shyly on the floor
and you had sleeved yourself into their press,
duct-taping the door against the light.

Wedged in your spandrel,
making an arch of yourself,
you dipped paper into three basins
whose acid smarted the air.

Sometimes you let me
squeeze with you into that sudden room.
The low hook for my coat jabbed my back
but I stayed dumb.

You conjured pictures from nothing,
smoked out ghost after ghost
staring up at me
by the amber safelight.

The brass bars were stripped of hangers.
The ceiling met my head and then yours.
Under the stairs was all angle and shadow,
and your eyes gleamed white as a miner's.

For a few years you unearthed moments,
clusters of smiles that shimmered out of the dark.

Under your careful eye,
our contours fleshed out slowly
till we bloomed like grey flowers
in your coal-cellar hothouse.

Then the chemicals
blistered your hands,
and you relinquished your dark room,
let garish prints come in the post.

But I held on to those minutes
when our lives took shape
in vivid monochrome
before you tore the tape away.

Outside the colour was superfluous
and the edges had no definition.

Pocket Knife

At the back of the table drawer,
behind his staple gun and nutcracker,
I find my father's knife.

Even a Swiss Army rookie would sneer
at this inheritance from my grandfather,
slender as a nail file.

From round end to square corner,
a hairline splits the mother-of-pearl casing
and there's a hole where a stud once shone.

I coax out the one thin blade
with its red-brown speckles,
but a small spike behind it resists.

Sitting by the window,
I worry the seized metal
till I get purchase with a dinner fork.

The spike suddenly eases out. I hear his voice say,
'That's for taking stones from horses' hooves.'
I never saw him use it.

I fold blade and spike
back into the handle
and wonder how many fathers passed this on.

Generations back,
it might have served Pegasus
or Niamh's fairy steed.

I slip it into my pocket.
All day I feel the pearly case,
smooth as sea-glass.

I finger the edge of the blade,
remembering my father's sharp eye
on the lookout for a lame horse.

Inheritance

for Mam

I don't care about the jewellery,
just leave me your litany of goms and eejits:

the big ignorant fostooks;
the lúdramáns thick as cudgels;
the useless collops plonked on the sofa;
the gligeens whose ears ache for a clip;
the leadránachs strung out like a long vowel.

Let me pocket your sly observations on
the corner boys acting the maggot;
the piscíns turning up their noses;
the long drinks of water;
the ones who would put years on you,
who wouldn't salute you,
wouldn't break eggs,
wouldn't smile if you gave them a ten-pound note.

I want to hoard your snide store
of tough women, targes and sergeant majors;
the pass-remarkables
who should be as smart at their lessons,
who would buy and sell you,
who would open your head.

Leave me your pity for the poor unfortunates:
the man you called Death Takes a Holiday;
the ones whose eyes aren't comrades,
whose feet are at ten to two;
the ones to whom you'd give tuppence;
the ones who haven't a ha'penny.

Mam, I don't care about the money,
just let me keep rattling
the loose change of your words.

The Shoe Box Coffin

My grandad, Joe, laid out his second son
in a card box from Donaghy's Boots and Shoes.
The priest said sacred ground was not for him:
the unbaptised. Joe's face was a dark bruise.
He knew about exclusion, had come south,
well rid of Turnabarson's beggared hill,
his kind long kept from housing and good jobs.
The priest, as he turned away, mentioned God's will.
That night, Joe's friends climbed the high graveyard wall.
Joe slid the box between the gate's grey bars,
threw in their spades and scaled the chilly steel.
They dug in silence under frosted stars
till Joe's hands placed, under the new-made mound,
the shoe box, secret in the sacred ground.

Naming a Bridge

for Rosie Hackett, the first woman honoured by a Dublin bridge

To make a bridge, you first must see the gap,
then fling yourself full-length across the space
like Rosie Hackett did for sixty years:
the factory girl who did not know her place.

Ah, Rosie knew that place and all its wrongs:
the sixty-hour week on the factory floor,
the union badge that barred her from her work,
the strike turned back upon the locked-out poor.

Her life's three struggles forged one steely frame:
the fight for women, workers and the Plough.
She raised a rebel banner from a roof;
for workers' holidays, she raised a row.

A name so nearly lost, now set in stone:
to name this bridge reclaims her for her own.

The Rebel Sisterhood

a street ballad for the women of 1916

Mammy, where did the women go,
When the men marched into the GPO?
Catherine Byrne, when a man said 'No!'
She looked at him and grinned-o.
With the help of two fellas in the know
Who hooshed her up from the street below
To a window-ledge of the GPO,
She jumped in through the wind-i-ow.
She jumped in through the window.

Granny, what was your position
When the fellas hoarded ammunition?
I'd a mattress stashed with armaments
And a gun in my undergarmaments.
I'd seditious notes in my piled-up hair
Tucked into a hat so debonair,
And I wore a smile and an innocent air
As I passed the British soldiers-o,
As I passed the British soldiers.

Tell me, what did the mothers say
As their sons and husbands marched away?
Some poor women were terrified
And they locked themselves and the girls inside.
But Mrs Byrne said, 'Do you have no pride?
Would you live forever occupied?
Go out and fight by your brother's side,
For we're equals in the struggle-o,
We're equals in the struggle.'

What kind of women, tell to me,
Went out to fight for liberty?
Counter assistants and a countess too,
Women like me and women like you,
There were straights with their mates who were best of friends,
Doctors, lawyers and thespians,
And we're still counting up the lesbians
Among the rebel sisterhood,
Among the rebel sisters.

Sister, what did the women say
When the men faced execution day?
Markievicz said, would you not shoot me?
Well I wish yiz had the decency.
For I didn't fight just for liberty
But for suffrage and equality,
So let us perish equally,
The children of the nat-i-on,
The children of the nation.

The One Who Shoots Stones

And he took his staff in his hand, and chose him five smooth stones
out of the brook, and put them in a shepherd's bag which he had,
even in a scrip; and his sling was in his hand.
—1 Samuel 17:40, King James Bible

Don't tell me you are David:
the one who chooses smooth stones
from the brook
and stores them in his pouch.

He is the one with the sling in his hand,
or with only his hand for a sling;
the one who flaunts no armour,
wears no helmet or sword.

It is not David
who controls the sky,
looms over the land with monstrous arms,
makes a shield of the earth.

That is the giant
who kills the first-born, the last-born,
the brothers and sisters,
the mothers and grandmothers.

Don't tell me you are David,
fighting fire with a flame,
the one who'll keep painting your wall
with the name you try to erase.

I think you will find
that if anyone
is battling the odds,
it is the one who shoots stones.

Sisters

a version of Child Ballad 10

I heard her foot slip on the slick stones
and I noticed nothing else
until the waterweed of her hair
floated past me towards the dam.

I thought the mill wheel
might catch her boot-cut jeans
and swing her into the open sky,
but it turned only water.

For weeks there was nothing but
white suits agitating the rushes,
'missing' posters, appeals for information
and CCTV shots from the local boathouse

until that busker
set up a speaker on the corner
and tuned the gold strings
on his ukulele.

His hands struck
over and over,
her high pleading
like blows on my ear.

The Man Who Was Not a Baker

Great-uncle George worked in a bakery
but his wife's lips drew tight
if we called him a baker.

'George', she'd say, 'is certainly not a baker.
He is a *confectioner'* –
as if a baker
was a drudge who churned out loaves,
while George was a milliner
turning edible hats.

Every Hallowe'en, packed in its own hatbox,
he sent the tall fez of his confectioner's brack,
studded with cherries
and gems of citrus peel.

Raisins polka-dotted the sides,
the top was varnished teak.

When my mother cut thick slices
to place on her gold-rimmed plate,
we'd scrutinise each piece
for hidden treasure.

Wrapped in small squares of greaseproof,
there'd be a ring or two,
a stick to beat us with,
a pea for poverty.

But we were filthy rich
with brack like a jewelled crown
made by Great-uncle George,
who was certainly not a baker.

Seven Works of Mercy

I. MIRACLE IN NAPLES
— *Feeding the Hungry* —

We make a pilgrimage
to the tiny chapel of Pio Monte della Misericordia
to feast on Caravaggio's *Seven Works of Mercy.*

It is our last stop in Naples
and the security guard, his keys already in the door,
is closing half an hour early.

We beg for one taste of our summer's last Caravaggio
and the guard tells us we can see it
on his black and white CCTV.

We squint in disbelief
as a side altar flashes onto the tiny screen,
next a dark rectangle, then a closed door.

The men who have been repairing the plaster
lounge under the porch,
their overalls freckled pinkish white.
Cigarette smoke trickling its haloes around them,
they wake to our pleading.

Suddenly the guard is centre of his own tableau.
At first the men are understated
but their gestures expand
as they shrug in our direction,
make a dumb show
of seeing, supplication,
disappointment, grand generosity.

Finally, with a sigh of defeat,
the guard unhooks the keys from his belt.
It is a miracle.

We crowd the space
before the altarpiece,
our eyes devouring Naples:
its madness, indifference, kindness,
crammed into one scene.

Had we not been four days in the city,
we might not have recognised
this realm of death and angels.

Above, Mary and her boy watch two seraphs plunge
towards a body carried past a dungeon,
while a woman casually suckles an old man
through the barred window.

And who would choose her to illustrate
feeding the hungry
and visiting the prisoner
but this jailbird painter with the dirty nails,
his blood maddening in the city heat,
a murder on his hands?

Where else could Samson
rub his Old Testament shoulders
with city slickers,
and drink from a bone
he holds over their heads
while beggars touch their feet?

Memento mori.
Before the guard can summon us,
we file out of the chapel.

II. DAUGHTER
   — *Visiting the imprisoned* —

I am breastfeeding my father through the bars.
My skin purses against the raw air,
my nose against the hum of death.
Mostly, the men ignore me.

I'm no novelty:
in Pompeii, a woman's ochre hand
holds a nipple to a wasted man
whose thin hand splays on her other breast.

Usually, it's the Madonna
whose breasts shower thirsty saints with miracles
but I am no virgin.

Even now, my eyes assess the crowd across the darkness.
A peasant grasping the shins of a corpse
tries to meet my gaze,
but I look beyond him at a possibility:

the innkeeper, in his goffered frill,
has an eye to commerce,
knows these passage-ways as I do,
can diagnose a situation.

This is no birth of the Milky Way,
no Rubens with lush cream exploding into a galaxy.
The heavens are unwinding like a shroud.
Only Caravaggio could capture me:

absence of hope in my swollen cheek,
the city's dirt cross-hatching my feet.
I am necessary and afraid,
a wet-nurse advertising my wares.

And Papa is no saint
made clear-eyed by a sprinkle
from the divine breast:
a runt who can barely suckle,
he dribbles onto his beard.
This, too, is love.

The nights pile up like detritus in the streets.
The angels' wings are dark, the fall is everywhere.
What looks like kindness is a kind of despair,
the knowledge of a shared fate.

His mouth depresses my breast.
Soon we will both be drained. Soon, again,
my feet will palpate the streets,
I will nurse only my bruises.

III. SAMSON
     — *Giving drink to the thirsty* —

What am I doing in this alleyway –
an antique rustic gawping in the town,
Samson Anachronistes, liquidator,
on whom immortal pity gushes down?

I am the one who showed no mercy, ever;
a God Almighty on a power trip;
a suicide bomber bringing down the temple;
the one who's lost and will not lose his grip.

I am the attitude without the buzz cut;
thick as a ton of bricks, the hardest chaw;
a long-haired layabout; a bible belter

laying about me with an ass's jaw.

I dip my bone in blood, paint only slaughter,
find mercy in a clenched fist squeezing water.

IV. PILGRIM
— Housing the stranger —

Shelter me.
I come from yonder or beyond,
on my hat the pilgrim shell:
cappasanta, holy hood,
or *pettina di mare,* little comb of the sea.

I tease out your motifs,
disentangle prejudice from better judgement,
raise or smooth down your hackles.
Shelter me.

I trawl coasts and borders with my scalloped edge,
panning for haven.
Shelter me.

I am the one he called
the least of his brethren
with the long thin face of Christ.
I am James navigating to the field of stars,
the hooded saint breaking bread,
the angel incognito.

I am your brother or sister.
Shelter me.

V. KNIFE EDGE
— Clothing the Naked —

You call me Caravaggio,
for the town where plague devoured my family.
I am on the run for murdering
a pimp because of a prostitute
and you ask me to paint
the seven works of mercy
for the church of the incurable?

At first I thought to cover seven canvases
with God's grace and man's charity
but time is a slash-hook to my days
so I crowd my misshapen pearls
onto one shell
for the altarpiece of the Pie Monte.

I am the master of tricks of light,
the cutting edge of chiaroscuro:
don't think I don't know
what gleams out of my baroque drama.
That luminescent blade
bedevils me continually.

I killed Ranuccio Tomassoni.
I tried to merely sculpt him into shape,
pare him down to panderer size, rasp at his jewels.
I thought I had him pinned
but he moved and the artery in his groin
bled his life out.

I am the memory of that raised sword
so, in a stab at contrition,
I wield my painted knife

to cut cloth rather than flesh,
sharing my cloak with a beggar,
not so much clothing the naked
as shrouding the wounds that gape at me now
from every sprawled frame.

All night, propped fully dressed,
I grasp the haft of my sword,
starting when my grip slackens.

I am the master of tricks of light,
but jab as I might
I cannot pierce this dark.

VI. CRIPPLE
— Visiting the Sick —

I twist in shadow past the rapier's gleam,
grimace almost invisible.
From down at the edge
I see the bigger picture –
what he is really at,
this oiler of patrons and canvases.

He got up this crowd
for the seven young nobles
who founded the church:
one act of mercy apiece,

but under the virtues
lurks a second seven:
the innkeeper's greed;
the woman's envy;
gluttony soiling her father's beard;

the lust of the falling angels;
the sloth of my strong companion;
the pride of the saint dispensing pity;
the wrath of Samson.

They are caught up in their passions,
sure of tomorrow and another chance.
They have not heard the rap
on the street door, the tavern window,
but in this town
sickness calls unannounced,
leaves its marked card,
stays on its own terms.

They do not so much visit me
as find me at their feet,
meet my jaundiced eye or not.

I am reading a doom
they will not heed
until the last day,
their sins
not deadly yet.

VII. VIRGIN
    — *Burying the Dead* —

They are brave as well as merciful
who'd carry a body through the streets
in these plague years.

In all of Merisi, you won't see a cleaner pair of feet.
Maybe he's washed the corpse of the man he killed
or perhaps it is me he lifts so tenderly.

Only last year
he splayed me bare-legged
in *Death of a Virgin.*

It was more a death of divinity:
a whore sat for me,
lay for me
across a doss-house trestle,
swollen-faced, dead drunk on cheap wine,
the picture of human suffering, certainly nothing divine.

The apostles, mouths slack with grief,
stewed in the shadows.
The light glanced off their pates,
caught my face in the lamp's full glare,
spilled over my ordinary body and unkempt hair
onto the lithe back of the Magdalene,
her fine linen sleeve,
the deft braids on her head.

Now and at the hour of our death

Despite my wire halo,
there was no hint of an assumption,
no incorruptible body,
no promise of resurrection,
nothing but a bed, a scarlet dress and drape
and a dish of vinegar to cleanse my cold skin.

Today, at least,
I am framed by wings.
I'm used to a gilt halo,
a coronet of stars,
at least a thread of light about my hair
but here my head is bare.

La Gioconda has nothing on me.
In my impassive mouth, my downcast eyes,
you'll read no emotion,
not for the world nor for the insolent angels
who hold each other as they fall.
How dare he conjure
their sensual embrace?

Me, I clutch my improbably blond child
whose full lips gleam out of his pallor
as he leans over the world;
with all my strength I hold him
lest he should slip.

from **A Bone in My Throat** (2007)

Meeting at the Chester Beatty

for Harry, one year on

We have only just met
Downstairs at the Chester Beatty Library
We have not touched each other yet

Upstairs Durer's *Adam and Eve* are contemplating
Each other and the apple
The serpent is already waiting

Upstairs are jars older than Grecian urns
Where lover strains towards lover
Fragments assembled so the hero yearns
Towards a clear plastic mould
A stopgap in scuffed images
Whole stories cannot be told

We have not yet become curators of ourselves
Guiding each other through halls of memory
Reading the small notes by the shelves

You have still time to discover
There are whole sequences lost from mine
Here or there, a missing line or lover

Upstairs is story within silken story:
Silkworms who shot threads like tiny roads
Were miniature cartographers of glory
For emperors who mapped their own silk routes
To carry gleaming bolts of gossamer
In colours of dreamed forbidden fruits

And we have not yet
Set up paths to each other carrying bolts of brightness
We have only just met

Upstairs are fabulous creatures with horns
In Cantimpré's *On the Nature of Things*
Monsters with benign faces, unicorns

Upstairs Isabella's marriage contract has no seal
Though holes gape where a ribbon might thread through
Louis loved another and thought better of a deal
That would have sealed up a century of war –
Blood ribboning between England and Flanders –
Love pounded louder than a battle's roar

Everywhere there is love and contract
Upstairs in the Chester Beatty Library
Where we have not made contact

Downstairs only our eyes have met
Beneath the weight of silks and histories
We have not touched each other yet

Lasagne

for Harry

It takes all day.
It builds like a story told over and over.

First the dough:
The eggs, amalgamated by slow fingers, gild the strong flour,
Your manly work-out of kneading
Rattles our ramshackle kitchen
Till our table boasts a golden ball
Casually: a prop for a fairytale.

Once upon a time
Your mother sat at her window
Rounding up thoughts with her pen
Rolling them onto white pages

Next, you start the sauce:
Brown the sausage till its sweet scent of fennel deepens;
Caramelise whole heads of garlic;
Dice onions, crush tomatoes, tear basil and rosemary;
Start the mesmerism of stirring
Till a crimson promise simmers on the stove.

Once upon a hundred times
You watched her begin like this,
Until she left it in your hands
To stir her days into words.

Once the dough has rested,
You roll it thin as cotton,
Cut it into broad ribbons,

Drape it on hangers
Suspended from doorknobs, dresser, drawer-handles.

The kitchen's a haberdashery,
A place of frills and furbelows where you measure out the cheeses:
Muslin-coloured Parmigiano,
Silky mozzarella,
Ricotta white as a bridal.

Once upon a time
She laid out pages on the study floor
Getting the order right
Adding the final flourishes

Now the layering, mumbled like a mantra:
Pasta, sauce, cheeses; pasta, sauce, cheeses;
And the reverent slide of dishes into oven,
A spell cast for a perfect marriage.

The story is coming to an end.
Her desk sighs as she closes it.
The stairs sing under her feet.
She is smiling her beautiful smile across the heat
And you smile back, the same smile.

Long before they taste it, our guests are lifting up their faces.
They are breathing in
Generations of Sicilian kitchens.
And when their full mouths murmur
That you have done it again, made everyone's favourite lasagne,
I taste love on my tongue,
Familiar as a household tale.

I am stirring our days into words.
You are smiling your beautiful smile across the heat.

Waiting for Olivia

for my sister Pat and her daughter Olivia

*You knit me in my mother's womb; I am fearfully and wonderfully
wrought. – Psalm 139*

While we are waiting, our mother marks time with her knitting.
All evening, her needles tick and flicker while a shape blooms on
    her lap.
A blue ball falls, spinning, when she takes a nap.
We used to squirm when she wound a skein on our arms,
    gritting
Milk teeth at being tied. Daddy cradles his guitar, his tone
Struggles to milk from mind a stream of song, keeps losing time,
And I sort old books: A child's history tells in rhyme
How early man stitched skins together with needles of bone.

Last night I dreamed of the child your womb is making:
In the dark, blood makes love to bone, flesh waking.

At dawn, we are still waiting for a storm to split the night
When down the passage of time comes a roar like thunder.
A woman is holding her work up, up to the light,
And the world is round with wonder.

Colours

for Tom, on his second birthday

Lello was your first, your pop-up sun
That cast no shade, however long it shone;
Your dayglo beach, so vast you could ignore
A line of blue that never rushed the shore;
Your chick, new-cheeping by its snow-white shell.
We proffered rainbows, but your only yell
Was *'Lello!'* Now you mouth blue and white with confidence.
Convinced you have outgrown a desk your size,
You perch at the edge of a bigger world, the kitchen table
    continent
Your armies of books and crayons colonise.
You colour in jaunty universes, tongue
Poised to give us your own take on them,
Scorning the green for grasses you have stung
Blood-red, scoring rich life on every stem.

Twelve

for Louisa's 12ᵗʰ birthday

Twelve is a foothold in a foreign town;
A ledge you lie on to look down
On childish things, and out at you-know-what;
Bras whether you need them or not;
Knickers and nerves to get in a knot.
Twelve's a bridge from end to edge;
The wafer of the grown-up wedge;
A walk with a hint of hip;
A mouth that gives everyone lip
Glossily; a fossily child in a woman's stone;
A bitter pill with bright pink sugar on it;
A whole poem, two lines shy of a sonnet.

Family Crest

Emblazoned on the coat of arms
My forebears bore into the fight
A mermaid grooms her golden hair
Mirror in left hand, comb in right

Certainly there's a family streak
Of that moist-voiced aquarian teasing
The siren luring men to rocks
In late night bars, the singing without ceasing

I'm not a blonde but fair enough
I take long baths, sometimes they last all day
The scales have not yet fallen from the eyes
That watch me go my pink-skinned-seeming way

I never wear jeans or trouser-suits
Prefer my clothing piscatory
That gleam of silver shoes beneath my skirt
Might be of something dreamed out of a story

Or could it be my only fin's
A *fin de siècle* fecklessness
Born out of long landlubbery
And consequent shipwrecklessness?

Stripping

I'm stripping the paint from the kitchen door.
Colours blister up and vanish like bruises.
Through the purple and orange blow-torch sparks,
Each shade of childhood bursts, diffuses:

Where we cried for exits and entrances;
Caught impatient fingers;
Pressed our ears to the grown-up talk;
Cracked nuts in the hinges;
Sobbed into the grain with slapped legs;
Slammed, or shut like a held breath;
Leaned long with lovers and exchanged
The kiss of life or death.

I am so lost in the lips of one,
My eyes smarting from the sparks,
That I forget you playing in the garden
While I scorch away the marks.
When I look up, your scarlet frock
Is a bright splash on the lawn,
And you are naked, crouched at a puddle
Of the early spawn.

I think to shield you from something
But before I shout
I am blind at the flash of your knees running
And the sound of your laugh brings out
A sudden terror of your beauty:
Head, a dandelion clock unblown;
Eyes, violet sparks not yet fallen;
Body, white as a bone.

How long is my hand burning
Before I feel it complain?
We were bred to offer up suffering,
Save souls with our little pain.
And I, who have no god to pray to,
Feel my heart cast a pagan spell:
That, not crying out, I will save you
Three blows, three bruises or three days of hell.

That a hand raised to you might suddenly drop,
A lover turn back before you wake from sleep,
And a door shut, soft as a whisper,
On a secret you shyly keep.

I am stripping the paint from the door where my heart has grown
And I have stripped the white deal down, to the bone.

Flashback

The green beam of old photocopiers
And the hot smell of that slow skim over glass
Rolls me back to a faded version of myself.

I am four years old.
Some virus has sprinkled my face with warts.
Mirrors show a marked copy of the original.

The treatment is a green lamp in a room
At Crumlin hospital.
A nurse ushers me in, seats me on a stool.

She wraps a pair of goggles around my head –
Brown rubber frames with green glass lenses
That turn me into a pioneer of air or sea.

She leaves me there, drawing a curtain behind her
And only then a green lamp flares to life.
Look! No safety net, no belt, no tank of air!
I am soaring alone into the green sun;
I am just stepping outside onto the moon –
I may be some time;
I am moving slowly under a green sea;
I am a plant synthesising chlorophyll.

Perhaps the lamp isn't green at all.
Maybe the viridescence comes from the goggles.
But there is a smell – the warm scent of green light.
I am the first to discover it.

I wait, staring at the lamp, till the nurse rings a bell.
Then I slide from the stool and emerge from behind the curtain.

That was my first quiet time.
I don't know how long I sat, bathed in leafy light,
But there was a sort of meditation in the glow,
An emerald city where I was wizard and Dorothy,
An altar where I worshipped once a week
Lit by my sanctuary lamp.

The warts went with the glow, or of their own accord.
For a long time I forgot it had happened.
Until one day our school got a new photocopier.
You fed in a page and the copies came out slowly
Inked in violet
Pockmarked with tiny flaws.

And as the green flashed over pages
I flashed back onto a stool in my first quiet room,
And all that day my mind ran off copies
Of my pockmarked face becoming clearer
Under a chartreuse moon.

Roundabout

The roundabout was the centre of our childish compass.
We took our bearings from the four roads it spawned.
When people asked the way it was part of the answer.
We crossed it on every journey.
Even the directions to our house depended on it:
'Four doors from the roundabout on the right-hand side.'

It was an island with a real Man Friday:
At the hub of its wheel,
A deserter from the British army
Had improvised a tent.
Old Tom played house
In a bivouac of canvas over sticks,
And boiled tea in a can with the milk and sugar stirred in.
In vain our mothers warned us not to beg a cup –
Tom's tea was our most exotic beverage,
Fiercely flavoured, black and smoky,
The lapsang souchong of our childhood.

The roundabout floated up to us like a life belt –
Before the traffic was a river in spate
We sat on the striped edge
And sank our summer toes in the tar-lines.
When the tar was soft and sticky
We dared ourselves to chew it –
Scooped fingertips of the melting gum
And blackened our mouths in a liquorice conspiracy
So outlandish it was not even forbidden.

The roads clogged up with cars and Old Tom
Moved to a building site behind the shops.
We mourned his loss, saw that change might come.

We were a flat earth society
Aware that we might fall off the world.

The roundabout became our circus ring
Where we juggled experience, experiments, excuses;
Our showjumping arena
Where we put imaginary horses
Through their paces,
Tested the water jumps,
Fell at the first hurdle;
Our stage where the light faded down slowly on summer
      evenings.

As we grew it shrank away.
The roads widened and withered our green circle.
A floodlight stole the shadows.

Now there are proper places to cross the four roads:
Sterile islands with plastic bollards
Which direct even your eyes away from the abandoned centre,
Where the ghosts of our small selves
Are stranded forever
In a dream of smoked tea and tarred fingers.

Oyster Girl

an 18th Century visitor to Ireland saw girls, naked from the waist down,
gathering oysters on the east coast.

I'd wade in seaweed to my waist
And feel the soft suck of the earth
Out where the teeming waters baste
Bare arms that pluck their suppers' worth.

Where I'd plough my watery acre
Shells that strain the ocean hide
Spinning otherness to nacre
Breathing in and out the tide

I'd haul up on the shore at night
My love and I would lie as tight
As two halves of an oyster's skin
I'd whisper glimpses of the girls
We'd let each other's strangeness in
To harden slowly into pearls

Cicatrice

The red moon scar that gaped on my thigh
From the barbed wire fence
Is waning.

At night I feel the itch of its healing,
Darn of flesh,
Stitch of cicatrice.

It was our last day by the river.
I stepped over the fence,
Feeling for a foothold on the other side, not knowing
The sure post under my back foot would yield
And one sharp knot of wire
Let rip a curve of flesh.

Your hand, stretched out for the last time, was not enough to
    save me
From this red stream turning to
A dried-up riverbed.

Under the remembering, a forgetting
Of that gasp of sharpness;
Under the forgetting, a remembering:
Hatchet buried like a trophy, lesson learned.

Like other scars, this will become
A hallmark of my mettle.

Other hands will trace the silver crescent.
Other eyes light on this moon in
My body's galaxy of bruised stars and planets.

And I will tell, or not tell, how your grey eyes,
Your face, the feel of your hands, have sunk,
Have been submerged in my flesh and stitched over.

In Memory of Frank Harte

Oh where oh where is the voice of Frank Harte?

When he sang there were two crowds:
One that gathered to listen and one he conjured out of the air.
He peopled the streets with Zozimus and Moses,
Summoned Billy in the Bowl,
Launched a flotilla of ships up the Liffey
Led by the Calabar.

Dublin made him and he in turn
Built his city out of old songs,
Resurrected heroes, restored lost bridges
So the ghosts could cross back to us.

As a child he heard old soldiers from the Dublin Fusiliers
Who'd gone from Chapelizod out to Flanders,
And they talked of killing snipers
In a place that they called 'Wipers'
And Frank sang of all the lives that battle squanders,
With his whack fol de di dol right tan tan te nah.

His voice was anguish echoing in an empty cell,
His voice was a keening for dead trades and dreams,
His voice was a passion kept in check,
Or a rebel blast across shivering rooftops.

His forest was willow and holly and laurel:
Trees where men were hanged,
Where birds told fates,
Where lovers were blessed or betrayed.

Oh where oh where is Frank Harte now?
He is sat fornenst a hawthorn bough;

He's unlocking Kilmainham, he's opening Mountjoy,
He is sending home safely a rosy-cheeked boy,
He is following someone he called Henry Joy,
Sing whack fol di die dol right tan tan tena.

He sang of lost worlds with lost words:
Tabinets and twangmen,
Waxies and swaddies.
There was a love that laughed in his telling
Of a scrimmage in Kimmage,
A rumblin' in Crumlin,
Of oul' wans and bould wans and blackguards and all.

He remembered the lot of the labourin' man:
The wasted navvies, the Paddies hoking spuds,
Those who held hods, turned sods,
Were crushed under wheels
Of industry or state.

He called up James, he called up Jim,
When history lived, it lived through him,
With failures, achievers
With lovers and leavers
To the whirr of the loom of the Liberties weavers.

Oh what will he leave us?
The sun and the moon,
And the air when it carries an old Dublin tune,
Sing whack fol de dirol die all the day long,
Sing Frank Harte the weaver has spun his last song.

Cherries

a villanelle for Katie, in memory of Phil

The ripened cherries roasted where they grew
Each fruit a blood-red world that shrank to brown
When the call came, I went at once to you

The orchards that last month you wandered through
Burst into sweetness as I left for town
The ripened cherries roasted where they grew

I prayed it wasn't, knew it must be true
Packed peaches for you with my mourning gown
When the call came, I went at once to you

This year there'll be no bottling to do
No *eau de vie de cerise* to lay down
The ripened cherries roasted where they grew

It was too late, however fast I flew
To share your last felicity or frown
When the call came, I went at once to you

We harvested the figs, the almonds too,
The golden plums that weighed the branches down
The ripened cherries roasted where they grew
When the call came, I went at once to you

Hedges

Not for us to thwart those who might scratch a living:
Born out of blackthorns straddling ditches,
We threw up our stark blooms in the unforgiving
Spring, grew the master's hazel switches

But found a soft spot for his mitching boy.
Made hiding room, nothing if not creative,
Wound rhododendrons in Traveller's Joy,
Let fuchsia from South America go native.

Let them flaunt style and stigma, take their chances,
Scatter their seeds into our multiculture,
Hazard our border hops and crossroad dances:
We back the underdog-rose, shading thrush from vulture.

Some of us, pruned now to inhospitable lines,
Embraced all comers once, flung wide our arms,
Grew spells for wives and witches, wove them signs:
Bad 'cess the hawthorn, rowan against charms.

Hedge schools, rebel priests, many a baggy britches
We've sheltered from bitter weather.
We are community, the thin silk that stitches
The threadbare fields together.

Winter Solstice

Passage grave at Newgrange

The chamber's heart is thrown a line of light
Once in the year. Out of the darkest days,
Astronomy, arithmetic effect this bright
Miracle, turning cold light to blaze,
Grey tomb to womb where a new year is kindled.
Heart, drink your fill of light: the darkness dwindles.

Introvert

From above,
a spiral staircase spins
inwards, downwards,
curling towards the centre of itself.

Run backwards the film
of a pebble tossed in water:
rings shrink and shudder,
one inside another,
contracting into one small stone
that leaps back to my fingers.

I am turning down the narrow stair
where only one can step:
there is no room to pass.

I am reeling in through the air
a dark stone
that makes no splash.

Butcher's Block

Officials have condemned the butcher's block
That fills up Hogan's shop on Wexford Street
But Hogan's standing square against the shock.
We passed this morning as he carved a side of beef.

Three old men stood around the block's rude form
Like druids around a fire. Maybe they knew
The Latin for hearth: *focus*. It kept them warm
To find this focus of community, chew

The fat of days, eyeball Hogan's skill
With giblets, gigot chops. This slab is no
Mere chopping board, it's a place of pil-
grimage, of grisly business and bloody show.

He is in love with his block, this scroll
That records his history. He keeps it from the wet,
Grooms it twice a day like a beloved foal,
The homely runt turned into family pet.

There is a map in his head. He traces the border
Between flesh and bone, knows veins and guts
Like the back of his hand, sees the order
In a carcass, the victualler's litany of cuts:

Skirts, scrags, saddle, chitterlings, crubeens,
Ox-cheek, -tongue and -tail, brisket, tripe, drisheens.

His Dad and Granddad wielded cleavers here
But Department health inspectors have no truck
With ghosts that crowd a meatblock. It is clear
To them the slab's already a dead duck.

His block is the heart of his trade, its staple.
He'll not mince words to keep it in his shop.
The block dreams of moose (it is Canadian maple)
While Hogan dreams of giving officials the chop.

Stepmother

From the point of view of the stepmother,
no fairytale has a happy ending.
Her lot is all suspicious looks in the mirror;
iron shoes reddening to a fierce glow at the wedding;
scarlet lips bitten against her scorching feet
as she dances straight-backed
till she drops.

After all, she only wanted what was best for her own two,
and the sight of the lovely, unimaginative stepchild,
servile, forever wolfing humble pie,
must have stuck in her craw.
You'd have trouble with it yourself.

She drove the action like an enormous engine,
blasting out balls and fairy godmothers
because the story needed them,
and thinking nothing of slicing off a heel here, a toe there,
to shape her shortcut to the palace.

And even when she's allowed a happy-ever-after
in the versions where she's forgiven
by those dull as they are beautiful,
it's only on condition that her fire is choked,
and she has to look on, smouldering,
while someone without a titter of ambition
purrs on and on, like the engine of a miniature train.

Half a Loaf

Obviously it was better than no bread,
but it never seemed right
for a mother to make her child choose
a loaf without her blessing
or half a loaf with it.

Some of them are obsessed with control,
with making you say, *I love you,*
or, *Your love is more precious than anything,*
the fairest of them all.

The two older sons always chose the full bannock
and who could blame them?
One loaf wouldn't last a day of their journey.
They'd likely starve before they found their fortune.

The youngest son, always his Mammy's boy,
took the half with the blessing of her whited hands,
confident of being spoilt with titbits along the road,
the world being no different outside home than in it.

His birthright would be more than
a mess of dough proving on the sill,
but those born first and second
needed a full stomach for their failure.

I never understood how a mother,
unfairest of them all,
could give two of her three cursed bread.
Ours would have given all six of us
the full loaf, with all her heart,
and the bite out of her mouth, instead.

The Children of Lir Quintet

LIR

I thought that I could fold away my grieving:
If Niamh's soft shadow blessed
My head on her sister's breast;
I'd feather a new nest, set my love weaving
White tapestries to crown our feather bed:
Four children stitched in silk
The ghost who been their milk
And Aoife, deep as lake water, quick in her stead.

And I was right to fear no vengeful shade.
It was a living heart
That bid the haunting start
And made my world, my warm-fleshed children fade.
You have undone me, Aoife,
I thought I was done with grief.

FIONNUALA

That sudden flurry of snow
Was more than a change in the weather.

As she shrieked the storm together
My soft lips shaping 'no'
Were lacquering to a beak.

Where I flung out my arms
To keep us from harm's
Way, was it a freak
Of the light or could I see

Feathers, the tips of wings?

And the three fledgling kings,
Who just now turned to me
My brothers' human eyes
Those heads born to be crowned
All down, all of their highness downed.

Too late now to be wise.

From mortals set apart
Left only human words
In mouths hard as a bird's
But harder still the heart

Of her who iced our tears
Half woman and half wizard
Who conjured us this blizzard
To storm nine hundred years.

AOIFE

Back then it seemed that something had to change
Before what love Lir felt for me was gone
I did not mean to make the whole world strange

Spells cast to bring together can estrange
Hardship recalled seem almost halcyon
Back then it seemed that something had to change

There was no robbery. A fair exchange –
Each white-faced child transformed into a swan
I did not mean to make the whole world strange

The dreams I had would any mind derange
Four babes that bit the breast they fed upon
Back then it seemed that something had to change

What happened was the best I could arrange
I sought to gain only what I'd forgone
I did not mean to make the whole world strange

Too late, I saw I'd reached beyond my range
And damned the very love I'd wished upon
Back then it seemed that something had to change
I did not mean to make the whole world strange

NIAMH

Jealousy clouded my sister slowly
Like the spreading of white wings
It fanned out over her, obscuring the sky

His love for them should not have shaken her
But she wanted his power to herself
Wanted no other mouth to kiss him
No other voice to call him from his work

She shrank as his love grew, till her heart
Was a pent-up bird
A nightjar with a dead wing

A barren woman bent on giving birth
For months she sat upon a monstrous egg
To hatch four swans out of my broken brood

She thought that she could launch herself
On borrowed feathers
That turning others into birds would give her wings
Her heart, waned by jealousy, waxing again
As she soared near the sun

It was white hot, her rage at their father's love
White as a swan or the foam on a cold sea
White as the sun on a waxen wing

Hers was a long torment
A beak that pecked and hissed through all her nights
A long neck snaking into all her dreams

CONN

They never get it right,
Those paintings
Foregrounding four snow-white birds
With Aoife seething on the shore behind.

We were only children.
We sat giddily on one side of the carriage
Eight small feet in a row
Like a simple sum.

Aoife sat opposite with her court shoes and her casket
Her eyes bent to a book of symbols
Calculus, she told us when we asked

She certainly was calculating something
A sort of long division

Of us four from our father
And, if she'd known it, of herself from him

I'd only begun to stumble through my letters
I could not read her face
But I did wonder after how she thought
She could subtract us and multiply his love

She took notes with a quill that scratched our hearts
And a dark plume smoked out
Of her hat of green velvet
It was the last feather in her cap

And as I was saying about the paintings:
There were no white swans that day.
We started out as cygnets
Stains on the green-eyed lake
Stubble-feathered, the colour of mud or sackcloth

Aoife's face was ashen
Now her long passion had passed
Paling at what she had done
She was the only white thing

TABOO

25 Sonnets on the Forbidden
in Myth and Story

TABOO

Don't:

Unlock the door
Let anyone in, any more
Eat the ripe fruit, open the box
Let your foot touch the floor

Because you will:

Let in the evil, let out the evil
See the bodies of those you understand
Taste hatred in a gleaming apple
Be older than death, alone in your own land

Song of Eve

I was dreaming of fire when I heard the apple calling me
Her voice was like water, cool and sweet and wild
Quenching my thirst, and my dream where an angel was flaming
Flowed the voice of the apple, a mother crying out for her child

There was no sound but the cry of the fruit, and the breath
Of the man who slept by me like a brother
We had no children then, and the wail on the wind
Was the voice of the apple, a child crying out for its mother

I followed the voice to a globe that gleamed under the moon
Like a beautiful breast on the tree
I am your mother, it said, *and my flesh is like milk*
Through it, all I know will pass to thee

I reached up my mouth to my mother
What did I know? I had no other

Apple

We weave a song beneath our skin
A spell to draw each other in
To where we both desire to be
One with the flesh, one with the tree

I need no lure in serpent form
I am the apple and the worm
Am what you sow and what you reap
The trysts and secrets that you keep

My secrets – knowledge, guilt and sin
Are useless if I hold them in
Eat of my flesh and set them free
But as you reach your mouth to me

Which of us hears the sweeter strain?
Whose is the loss and whose the gain?

Adam

I was lonely and lost for words to put flesh on my wish
Though the sun spilled shimmering seas of greenish light
Till God plucked a wishbone from my ribs one night
And Eve dived out of His dreams like a fabulous fish

World made in seven days, in one made fresh
The early sky bloomed red as lips that morning
But what cared we for any shepherd's warning
Who burned our thumbs on pink-as-salmon flesh?

Eden opened, my oyster, with Eve its pearly centre
His own peep-show shut out that Mad Inventor
Who spawned free will, while brooking no dissenter

Oh, luscious fruit! We did not count your cost
Till, writhing on the sand where we were tossed
We gasped for air or water or whatever we had lost

God

An apple on a tree I dreamt
A world to try, a world to tempt
No time, and all, it took to fashion
And half my power and all my passion

Only one rule for them to break
I made. There could be no mistake
An apple that was meant to bless
Exposed them to their nakedness

The dream was both the seed and yield
An angel with a flaming shield
And in my dream man's fate was sealed

For I had made the apple first
Into the void its sweetness burst
And nothing else could slake their thirst

Serpent

I merely asked if ignorance was bliss
The question was rhetorical, of course
But hardly served to justify all this
Well, shall we say, unreasonable force?

God set a task no creature could fulfil
Not that he could admit his own mistake
To couple with conditional free will
The choicest fruit, the choice they must not make

Though no good comes without a hefty price
I still believe it was my finest hour
I had to show God how to sacrifice
I had to teach man how to challenge power

They ate the fruit and ate away my feet
As though I said, *My body: Take, and eat*

Zeus

Prometheus gave to men immortal fire
And set my heart ablaze. Man would acquire
His flames from me: hot rage, the scorch of lust
A burning girl to spin their gold to dust

The gods gave her all the gifts they could bestow
Beauty that lit in her a candle-glow
A lake of charms where all men longed to float
Kindling a desert thirst in every throat

More godmothers than gods, they read no rift
In her christening, no malicious gift
No sense of finger or of conscience pricked
No portent of the great hall derelict

But I was the fairy left out of the feast
And in her beauty I would hide a beast

Pandora

I dreamed that I would lose and find myself
In the gold box that blazed upon the shelf
So I shut out the grave and glaring sun
Undid the clasp. Now the whole world's undone
The black air swarms like moths. I am the torch
That courts them, mine are the wings that scorch
What can I dream now, in the furnace roar?
That fire be a hearth to gather round, once more?
That man and child with love will speak my name
That now men spit, though phlegm can quench no flame?

The burning lock I cannot mend
I do not know where it will end
I did not know that it would start
This breaking open of the heart

Jar

The jar's already full of cracks
She's hot enough to melt the wax
The world wanes as she breaks the seal
Nor heads nor hearts will ever heal

The gods abhor a lovely woman
They had their plan: She had it coming
Their gift was but a can of worms
Look in its mouth, but on their terms

Before her voice was ever heard
Men saw her, and their lust was stirred
Before a woman's word was spoken
The seal on every heart was broken

Men, do not blame her as you leer
For you are everything you fear

Gods

Did they unlock their death? We hardly care
Mortals are of such little consequence
But it amused us once to watch them bear
The sense of loss amid the loss of sense

Who, given wings of wax, could fight the wish
To soar too close to the forbidden star?
To taste the fatal fruit, the fickle fish
Or break the seal of the avenging jar?

Heaven shaped jar and girl to wake desire
And into one breathed blood, the other fire

Both fashioned out of clay, gifts from a stranger
Long-necked, round-bellied, hard to tell apart
Even the gods know not which holds more danger
The ignorant or the malignant heart

Hope

Out of a world struck dumb what starts, what starts to stutter?
Out of the empty box, what heart breaks, what wings flutter?
For those bankrupt of dreams, what gleams in the gutter?

Your stumble through the darkness has begun
I am the voice that says you can outrun
This flight of evil birds across the sun
For of the ills unleashed into the air
I will not let the greatest be despair

I am the life that stirs beneath the rubble
However crushed, I will be worth your trouble

Though currents drag you to the ocean floor
I am the wave that flings you towards the shore

In the shroud's pockets, I the precious token
The words of love, though no more words be spoken

Salmon

You leapt a waterfall to spawn
Your flesh the pink of every dawn
The portent of a sky at morning
A boy's delight, a druid's warning

Year after year that upstream ride
Against all odds, against the tide
You knew too much to fall for bait
With rainbow scales you lay in wait

Those held no promise for Finnegas
(He thought you gift, but you were magus)
Unless there is a sacred place
That's reached by not achieving grace

You blistered so a boy would come
To burst a bubble with his thumb

Finnegas

I caught an image in a golden pool
And thought me favoured, though I was a fool
To learn your salmon seasons and your seas
To watch you savour fruits of fairy trees

Learning was all my salt and all my spice
The taste of truth, my dream of paradise
And I was Eve and Adam with their thirst
To drink all knowledge in, to be the first

What was that scent of wisdom on the air?
Quicksilver silver, fair and not so fair
Bitter my sentence when at last I knew
That scent came from the youth and not from you

Yet there was mercy in your shining scales
What learns more fully than the heart that fails?

River Speaks to Finnegas

There was a catch, you thought, hauling your salmon in
All your long life reeled in that leap of joy
Flashed in the flame that lit it from within
Why did you trust it to a burning boy?

For it was you who floundered, gasped for air
You who was caught with your own instrument
You whose consuming dream devoured you there
You who was heft out of your element

Rivers see everything, snaking from God's own garden
Making falls, floods, watching man fish and flail
Feel in our waters when to melt and harden
How to change course when old directions fail

But this was new: to yield without a word
To banish none, brandish no sudden sword

Fire Speaks to Finnegas

You came back, hungry for your dish of learning
To find you had been nothing but the bait
Seven years to hook a fish, your days' dreams turning
Black on my spit, your life a wasted wait

A twisted prophecy stuck in your craw. It
Said a white-haired man would gain the prize
But even before you looked at Fionn you saw it
That hurting brightness blazing from his eyes

Where is your rage? You too were *fionn*, were fair
Turning away now, turning the other cheek
How is it you could watch all of your share
Slip from your grasp, which took your life to seek

And call a blessing on your torment, as you turned
As though there was something greater you had learned?

Fionn

There is a taste of everything: the slip 'twixt mouth and dish
The skin shimmers, blisters on your finger and the fish

How could you ever hide that blinding spark?
Blood on a key is not so bright and plain
Like the knowledge that you are naked, stark
You never can scrub off that seeping stain

The world's sea washes through you
A leaping salmon spawning all, all seasons
Giving you all the human heart's gone through
Its terrors and its triumphs and its reasons

You alone escape unscathed with your prize
The women never did. Eve, Pandora, Bluebeard's wife
No kind man saw the changeling in their eyes
And said, *Take everything. It is yours, this life*

Oisín

You thirsted for the comfort of old faces
For eyes through which a softer sunlight shines
For speech oaked with remembered shades and places
For vellum skin, to read between the lines

You thought you could go back. None of us can
Not in this world where all that lasts is change
Giants dwindle, every boy becomes a man
When you're estranged, even your home grows strange

Yours was the first death that your wife would know
She begged you not to, knew you had to go

Life's sweetness is its shortness, all that's wasted
It cloys too much to be forever young
Shrivelling into yourself, at last you tasted
The thrill of honey on your dying tongue

Ireland

Come back! Though your past is crumbling, overgrown
Or bleaching on the hillside like a bone

Already I'm anointed with your blood
Red rivers ribbon every blasted field
While you, your life drawn out, believe it good
To bleed still, from landmarks that never healed

Remember, in this land for which you yearn
How you lay wounded, face-down in the briars?
The dust you ate shall eat you in return
But still my features crown all your desires

Touch me, and be at one with all you crave
One look will make you do what you've forsworn
My gravity will pull you to your grave
I draw out life as men draw out a thorn

Horse

Too much of anything is still too much
A glut of sweetness or a golden touch
For only yesterday you took Niamh's hand
And rode my splendour to an ageless land

But now youth pales and old age haunts your sleep
What if I span ten years with every leap?
What if my golden hooves tread silver foam?
Stones in your heart are still the stones of home

That soil you crave wastes every hero's life
And ravishes the beauty of his wife
Pulling its green around her like a cover
Pushing between her thighs like her last lover

Your land, your mistress is a fatal jade
One touch, and you'll be nothing but a shade

Witness

This place would put years on you, I heard Conn say
Then time snapped. The god was shrivelling away

His horse was already almost out of sight
Pounding the waves that glittered on the shore
As though he had opened some forbidden door
At dawn, letting in the darkest dead of night
Without bright midday or declining dusk
One minute, leaning like a golden god
Hoisting a rock as though it were a sod
The next, no hero but a human husk
He gasped out something with his dying breath
We didn't catch. His eyes were bright with tears
As though he'd been asleep three hundred years
And suddenly awakened into death

Ribbons

Niamh's Lament for Oisín

You cut my heart to ribbons when you left
Those strips of scarlet made the whole world wan
Your fingers so incisive and so deft
I never felt a thing till you were gone

Your scissors on the floor was a bad omen
The portent of a stranger or a death
In the mirror I faced another woman
Though I leaned close, I could not see her breath

I gathered up those ribbons in a tin
I wear them every morning in my hair
Some say the scarlet sets off my pale skin
Some think me proud of what I have to bear

But I, who could not make our love survive
In small scraps keep its memory alive

Bluebeard

When first they caught sight of my beard, all my damned
    pretty wives were afraid
But my eyes, sharp as axes, could see how my gold seemed
    to burnish the shade

Between my silk sheets they said sweetly
It was sapphire or azure or aquamarine
And they swore to be blinded completely
To that one room that could not be seen

They never fooled me for a second
It wasn't the bloody key, but the way
That they shrank when I beckoned
Them bedwards, always a dead giveaway

Curiosity killed them. They clawed like cats at the places
They knew were forbidden, the curse of their sex
The blood had already drained from their faces
When I touched their necks

First Wife

He liked me singing by the fire at night
He'd stroke my neck, but say my voice was flat
One night I thought his fingers held too tight
I went off-key more often after that

Good lovers must learn cruelty, he said
And mouths must learn to bite as well as lick
Had he a real woman in his bed
She'd know enough to match him, trick for trick

I heard the sizzle of an icy sea
I dreamed I drifted in a red-hot boat
I was a songbird in a blackened tree
And he found fault with every frozen note

In the end, there was so much he didn't like
Whether the iron was hot or cold, he'd strike

Door

Whatever you do, you must never open it

But in her heart it opens a thousand times
Swings in on terror, the creak of hinges
Unhinging herself. A dark stair climbs

Twisting, in her mind
To where everything says, *No Entry*
At all her exits and entrances
This one door stands sentry

Its threshold shifting under all her ways
As though it were made of fragrant applewood
From the first tree, it smelt of myth
And darkest dreams, and secrets, and cold blood

When she stands before it, confronting everything
The whole house trembles, opens, as the door roars in

Last Wife

I grew to like his beard, that turquoise mesh
That blue sea washing up on my white flesh
I never thought that I must float or drown
Till one room's secret weighed my body down

I dreamed that I was trembling on the shore
I dreamed a trickle underneath the door
The walls cried out, the door begged, *Let me creak*
Someday, someone who comes will live to speak

Our house was beautiful, a golden shell
Within its rooms I heard the ocean swell
But at one door at last I understood
That deafening tide: It was the roar of blood

The door cracks open with a shriek of pain
A damburst that no finger can contain

Brother-in-Law

His eyes were mouths that swallowed women whole
Those oyster-cool, those lovely, bone-white girls
Slipped down the dark, embittering his soul
He always tasted fish, expected pearls

Rumours like soot showered from a servant's flue
Said childbirth wasn't what had killed his wives
His hands were spotless, hearth and chimneys, too
Were scrubbed within a half-inch of their lives

He ate with relish, gave restraint no quarter
Fattened his pretty white geese for the slaughter
Not what you'd wish your sister or your daughter

We killed him, and our women's tongues were freed
They dug for the truffle of his darkest deed
And wolfed it down, as though they shared his greed

NURSERY RHYME

What are little boys made of?
What are little girls made of?
Sugar and spite
And heat in the night
And everything we're afraid of
That's what we are made of

from **Strange Familiar** (2013)

Three Sestets on Stories

I. ENLIGHTENMENT

All past reflections shimmer into one:
The apple where Eve's lonely contours shone;
mirrored in their blood, the murdered brides;
in the sea, a horse that one and no one rides;
the gold lid, closed and opened, where Pandora sighs
and drinking all in, giving all back, Fionn's eyes.

II. ESCAPE

In every human tragedy, you feature
among the scathed: the one who gets away,
the torment of the writhing, hollow creature
whose eyes ask only that you see and stay.
All that you've learnt has shrunk, just this you know:
when the enchantment breaks, turn tail and go.

III. URGE

Since there's no cure for curiosity,
you must reach out at last to what must be.
Be it a box, an apple or a land,
it craves the touch of mouth or foot or hand,
craves but the instant where, all past things flown,
the familiar shape-shifts into the unknown.

Three Poems for My Father

I. CUT OFF

My father worked with the Electricity Board.
He was a power surge that turned night to day,
made the streetlamps dawn pink one by one
and the yellow light leap down the street.

My father was plugged in to everything.
He was gadget man with his electric potato-peeling bowl,
his siphons, flares and phase testers,
his occasional swims against the current.

He said, *let there be light*, but sometimes hid his under a bushel:
At night the faintest glow kept him awake.
He made a lid to cover the digital radio clock.
Even the TV's standby light, he taped over.

He had delicate hands for the works of old clocks,
but on holidays complained of a grandfather chime in the hall
or a church bell that mourned the quarter hour:
He hated to hear time measured out.

On the night of his wake, we were suddenly cut off.
Floods separated the suburbs, the kettle stayed stone-cold.
His jerry-rigged system went haywire
and light buckled across the world.

II. ALWAYS NOT THERE

You are always
not there, now.
When I wonder about your grandfather's house in Turnabarson,
or who fathered a second cousin's child;
when three teenagers banjax the sofa-bed during the World Cup;
when a door scrapes the floor and needs shortening;
when it's a question of the best way to do something, to get
    somewhere,
you are always not there.

You were a problem solver.
There was nothing you liked better
than to look over your glasses at a broken thing,
till it provoked you into
reaching out the perfect tool
from your endless store of
pliers, tweezers, staple guns, wire cutters.

You could draw a plan of the *cúl tí* bed sat into the hearth,
write an encyclopaedia of family secrets,
draw a freehand map of Ireland,
get from here to Ringsend without passing a traffic light.

And we don't mind splitting the bill,
but we miss your sly pleasure in paying:
You were always at the table's head,
discreetly gesturing to the waiter,
keeping everyone's hands in their pockets,
at your happiest the day I told you
you were a great provider.

And what our eyes say now, when we meet
over celebrations and casual dinners,

is that the table looks off-kilter since
you are always not there.

III. THE GOD OF UNRAVELLING

My dad was the god of unravelling.
He unpicked the cord on brown paper parcels
while we begged to rip them open.
That's a grand piece of string, he'd say.

Flexes and wires he knew
like the knotted veins in his hands,
where each began, ended and intertwined
behind his big chair in the corner.

He was a dab hand at taking knots
out of gold and silver chains,
methodically smoothing the ganglions into strands
which he laid side by side on our polished table.

When we showed off our muscles,
flexing the small bumps on our arms,
he would assess them, and say with his slow smile,
I've seen bigger knots in thread.

My mother's bag of wool,
a spaghetti mess of blues and reds,
he would subdue into neatly rolled balls,
his thickened fingers worrying the nests apart.

He had no time for yoga or meditation,
but his busy brain calmed and lost itself
in the cool analysis of chaos,
the challenge of a tangle.

Pushing the Boat Out

for Síle Yeats

You will not sit across from me again
and smile, and say, *I think we'll push the boat out.*

These last years you gave house wines a wide berth,
went straight for the Sancerre or the Chablis.
Life's too short for the cheap stuff, you said,
Why don't we push the boat out?

Life was too short indeed for you,
so we who remain
are glad you lived for the moment
before you knew how few moments were left.

Remember the room you booked us in Milan? That four-star hotel?
Sure, why would we bother with the twin room, you said,
when the suite is a snip at eighty-nine euro?
We may as well push the boat out.

Few of the hotel clients – the impeccable suits, the stiff-haired
    ladies –
can have enjoyed it as we did:
We were charmed by the fake Louis Quinze chairs,
our marble sitting room,
the gold taps on the bath.
It was too lovely to leave,
so we saved on dinner by eating a picnic
on the pale silk sofas.

In London you went all the way to five star,
and blagged your way to a penthouse upgrade,
pushing the boat out like an old hand.

In the end you were too weak
to fight against the tide,
but your boat was pushed out so far
it no longer bothered with the shore.

Instead it bobs far out,
in its hold a bone-dry Sancerre,
a silver ice-bucket,
a plate of exquisite cheeses.

Its cabin is furnished
in no-holds-barred style:
Egyptian cotton sheets, eau de Nil throws,
a thick bathrobe with deep-pile slippers,
here and there, perhaps, a monogram.

You are in there now
listening to Verdi on the latest hi-fi,
a silver window opening on the foam,
the colour back in your cheeks,
the sea breeze in your hair.

It's a good job you had little faith in heaven:
Your map-reading would never take you there,
and I'm not sure how St. Peter would react,
if you gave him your best smile,
and asked him for an upgrade.

Contraband

I have smuggled it to England, France, Italy, America:
a brown slab wrapped in cling film
taking the space of a holiday read.

And indeed it has its share of stories:
Each time, the baggage x-ray slows, stops.
Its operator studies the dense rectangle,
tries to read it for herself.

It's my mother's brown bread, I say.
If I came without it, I'd be dead.

There is a dusting of flour underneath
so it won't stick to the roasting tins,
and only the roasting tins are big enough.

The crust is the colour of fudge, the inside a shade paler.
It looks solid but has a soft bounce of air.
It conjures up my mother's fingers barely touching the sticky dough,
in her head that elusive recipe.
Whenever we asked
she said, *this one was only thrown together.*
Something was missing or forgotten,
there'd been no buttermilk, or oatmeal.
When she made it properly, she'd let us know.

The pony-tailed security guard
calls her colleague over.
Once he's sure it is, in fact, bread,
he sighs and asks if I am carrying any other drugs or weapons.

I do not carry drugs or weapons,
but my knife was always ready

when the bread was slid from the oven.
In vain my mother wrapped the steaming loaf
in a checked tea-towel
to try to fend us off.

You'll garter it, she told us.
It won't cut till it cools down.
But we each hacked a ragged slice,
slathered it in cold butter.

It'll stick in your craw when it's too hot, she'd say.
We'd giggle, ask her where our craws were,
and ignore the ache between our lungs
where the warm dough lodged.

I do not carry drugs or weapons
but the bread contains a mind-altering substance,
distorts your perception of time and place,
brings you back ten, fifteen, twenty years
to the kitchen table, the smell of home.

I do not carry drugs or weapons
but my mother supplies this for free
even after you are hooked,
and on every journey you're a courier.

In England, France, Italy, America,
when I share my mother's brown bread,
it's familiar as an old book,
and old friends ask if I have the recipe yet.

I don't think I'll ever manage it.
There's some knack to the way
the table under our elbows becomes home
and the years dissolve in our mouths.

Strange Familiar

Not god nor devil brought you.
I neither chose nor own you,
but am bound to you by blood and wonder.

You were the dark shape at my ankles,
weaving between my feet,
one minute clawing the air, all arch and hiss,
the next a soft curl against my breast.

Time was, they might have burnt both of us:
me muttering snatches of rhyme,
you with your constant self-commentary,
your animal companions, your night terrors.

Now you look crooked at me,
your father's fire flickering your nostrils,
and I understand that though he and I
made ourselves whole together,
you made no such contract.

We're caught in that tit for tat:
I too was the spit and image of my father,
a strange familiar to my mother
whose eyes for me were all nonplus and puzzle.

My apron-string kitten,
it seems I turned once in a circle
and found you shapeshifted
to this long-limbed branch-leaper,
walking on air solid as earth,
blending fire and water,
always in your element.

I turn again and catch you
looking out of your Moorish grandmother's almond eyes,
eyes cool and clear as hieroglyphs of eyes.

Your skin, opaque as moonlight,
betrays something of your astral travels.

You are making yourself visible
without a spirit guide,
contained enough to conjure
your own familiar.

Grandmother Daedalus

Sunlight was the enemy of my maternal grandmother.

Earthed in the half-light of her kitchen,
she shunned the excess of the sky.
The shades were drawn in her parlour
so midday could not wilt the chintz roses
or spotlight the dust motes that soared accusingly.

Daily she scrubbed ceiling to cellar:
She could not fathom
how her rooms harboured floaters and feathers,
suspected that the sun created dust.

Sunlight was the enemy of my maternal grandmother.

She kept her pantry dark and cool
for the sun spoiled butter, milk, meat.
There was no end to the folly of those who courted it.

On hot days she drank scalding tea in the shade,
wore a battered hat as she beat dust out of carpets
and kept her face and arms covered,
for only labourers and washerwomen got a tan.
Even her front door wore a blind to stop its paint blistering.

Sunlight was the enemy of my maternal grandmother.

She shook her head when jetlines scored the summer sky.
When God wants me up there, He'll call me, she'd say.
He called her too early, and my child mind
could not imagine her solid form floating to any Heaven.

Now when I see the property supplements I think of her:
Soak up the sun in this light-flooded jewel.
Head above the clouds in this pied-à-terre.

I imagine her reading them in the time she never had,
twitching like a Roman blind with exasperation
and warning, *we'll all melt in this heat.*

The City of Chocolate

Chocolate is a fairytale
with ugly sisters feasting at the ball
and Cinderella working in the ash;

with the giant thundering above the stalk
and Jack and his mother going
from subsistence to starvation.

Chocolate is an exotic empire,
a city of dark squares and bitter streets,
an ancient democracy destroyed.

Mayans, rich and poor, drank the dark froth
till Aztecs turned their beans to currency,
their farmers to slaves,
their foam to an elixir.

We pluck it from a shelf,
unwrap the glossy paper, glitzy foil,
place a tablet to melt on our tongues
or snap it quickly and secretly.

They pluck the ripe pods, large as melons,
split and scrape,
spread seeds and pulp to dry in the sun,
then pack the yield, too precious to be tasted.

Chocolate is an ambiguous relationship,
the too-sweet encounter, the sharp aftertaste,
too much or too little
of a good thing.

Alone with its dark savour,

your mouth hears its own sound,
a soft hum that resonates
in your head and throat.

Chocolate is lexicon of exotic words:
Olmec, Izapan, Mayan, Aztec,
Tabasco, Yucatan, Guatemala,
a sound that began with X or K,
a kiss that we couldn't pronounce, a betrayal,
always harvested by the poor of one place
for the wealthy in another:

Remember as your hand
brings that exquisite square to your mouth
that some who live hand to mouth
built this delicious city.

And yes, there are princes
who fight dragons to set workers free,
and sisters who share the spoils
and giants who tumble down.

This is how the city's contours soften
how its heart expands and melts
till Jack's mythic, magic beans are worth a cow
and he can enter the City of Chocolate now.

White, Too

AJ: I thought black was death?
Meadow: White too.
– *The Sopranos*, discussing Frost's *'Stopping by Woods on a Snowy Evening'*

White too? There's not a colour can escape
The palette that no artist could eclipse
Your memory takes on every shade and shape

The silk that priests over your coffin drape
Like that you loved beneath your fingertips
White, too. There's not a colour can escape

The freesia petals hollow as the nape
Of neck that called out for my lips
Your memory takes on every shade and shape

The chalice filled with some beloved grape
Rhône red, that rosé you eked out in sips
White, too. There's not a colour can escape

The crematorium's grey curtains gape
And billow to the contour of your hips
Your memory takes on every shade and shape

The night you crumpled up your dress of crêpe
And melted, melting me.
                              The candle drips.
White, too. There's not a colour can escape
Your memory takes on every shade and shape

Black Stuff

I grew up near the Guinness houses:
Corrib Road, where no river flowed
but the black stuff, delivered in crates at Christmas
to ould lads proud of the grand job.
Guinness was good for them:
Arthur gave them their pension, fed their crateload of children
from pint-sized to full of bottle,
gave girls and boys alike their first moustache,
rented them houses till they could buy them out.

I like its colour, muddy as the Liffey;
the way its black and beige dust motes
separate, settle into coffee and cream
in the time it takes to tell a story, catch your breath;
its taste of roast and toast, that first sweet sup,
warm from the tap. You can't sup beer or lager,
that lightness on your lip
could never be more than a sip.

And porter carries many a conversation still:
no beer is so hotly debated, so coldly assessed:
The perfect temperature's a keg's worth of chat,
even the distance to the barrel
is worth mulling over.

Last year we found a short tap in Tralee,
settled like slow pints at a corner table,
and parted with the landlady like family.

What better drink for your last request?
No claret inking thin glass,
or brandy burning in a great balloon
could see you off like the contemplation

of those last slow breaths rising and falling
till the head stands proud of the body.

Stowaways

The woman around the corner
says country people are taking over Dublin.

She says you can see the return tickets
floating down the Liffey every Monday morning.
Country people are letting on they're coming up for the
    weekend,
then the cute hoors are stowing away,
getting jobs in the newspapers, running the civil service,
writing speeches for TDs
and signing grants for the relations.

I think of them crouched in the leaky hold of the city,
sharing a damp cabin with hard-up Dubliners.
or washed up in that bedsit that made me cry:
The room split in three with hardboard partitions
like a home-made doll's house,
the one window favouring the living room,
the kitchen and bedroom lightless,
the old landlord inviting me to sit
in a chair pushed against one wall,
my feet touching the blinded fireplace on the other
and tears itching my eyes.

For years I hoped whoever lived there
had some happiness to fall back on
and got out alive.

The woman around the corner
wouldn't trust anyone from outside Dublin.

Just because they're from two counties away
doesn't mean they're not immigrants, she says.

To be honest, she's not sure
about people from the northside either,
but as long as they cross the river again after work,
she says she's happy enough,
though she never looks it.

We Buy Gold

We buy your memories and heirlooms by weight.
They are worth much less than you think,
the family's gilded candlesticks,
or your great grandmother's rose gold wedding band,
engraved with her name and his.

In the photograph over the piano,
she displays it shyly against the home-made Charleston dress,
run up in secret after she took the original
home from the draper's on appro.

Her ring feels heavy on your hand,
but the long years you kept it safe
and got by without pawning it
weigh nothing to us.

Your mementoes are scrap metal.
We erase their individuality:
The names on the ring, the roses on the earrings.
We ungild your lilies and discard the flowers.

Those treasures that a line of daughters
massaged with soft cloths,
swaddled and tucked into boxes,
we merge with the heirlooms of others.

We subtract the weight
of stones you think are precious.
You do not have to remove them,
but we cannot take them into account.

Gravity exerts little claim
on your gold-plated crucifix.

We weigh sentimental value
and find it wanting.

We do what it says on the sign:
We buy yellow gold; white gold; rose gold;
wedding bands; engagements rings; chains; pendants; earrings;
bracelets; bangles; damaged pieces; dental gold;
coins; nuggets & bullion.

We won't encourage you
to prise the fillings from your teeth,
but if they happen to fall out,
we will certainly give you a price.

Time was, our business seemed shameful,
lurking down darker lanes,
but the age of recycling
has made us respectable.
We are brightly lit, we choose main streets,
we are all business.

We are reverse alchemists:
We may not turn your gold to tin,
but we show that your emperor
had you fooled all along.

We melt memories down
to their essential elements.
We don't deal in dreams or histories,
we buy gold.

Grange Abbey, Donaghmede

It's a shell marooned on a suburban shore,
a shell that we scarcely listen to:
Open your ears!

Under the tide of traffic there's a faint rush of sea;
the wind singing in the golden meadows;
the shouts of men hoisting keystones;
the stone-cutter at the grave slabs.

Here lies a way of life:
The church itself a gravestone now,
the graveyard a park, unloved as parks go,
a local traversy, a travesty
of stripped bicycles and shopping trolleys.

Here lies the Grange of Baldoyle:
A medieval supermarket, a busy farm
with daily deliveries on carts or foot
into the spreading town.

Open your ears!
Can you hear the King of Leinster's coach,
hear his great lungs breathe in the country air?
That's the scratch of his quill
gifting his gleaming fields to city monks.

Open your ears!
Hear the din of dinner at the Priory of All Hallows:
Trinity monks sup milk from Baldoyle cows,
feed on Grange cheeses, bread and butter,
quaff St Donagh's mead.

And we should drink deep from the well of history:
These walls guard secrets still,
have barely teased the archaeologists
with splinters of bowls and bones,
a riddle of shifted stones.

Open your ears!
A whole world quivers like a slammed door
in this shell washed up on a suburban shore.

Badger

I've never seen you alive:
You're from stories, riverbank tales
of a gentleman in a dinner jacket,
the solid citizen who prevails.

A mystery like your name:
Are you badged head or corn-hoarder,
or grey man, the Irish *broc*,
a fugitive living on the border?

Holing up in a dug-out,
solitary or thick as thieves,
covering miles in the night
to reach a safe house, eaves-
dropping on your foes without a sound,
giving no quarter when you clamp down.

Giant Panda

There was excess postage on the package
for the *Musée d'Histoire Naturelle*
Père David sent back from China
in 1896. Out of it fell

a monochrome pelt,
a skeleton and a few lines about amazing weeks
in the Himalayas, finding a raccoon-faced lumberer
in woods amid jagged peaks.

The bear with its dark spectacles in a white face,
the priest with his cassock, white collar and air of distinction,
both camouflaged in the dapple sun on snow,
all light and shadow, loners on the brink of extinction.

A carnivore turned vegetarian, barely surviving
on its own bodyweight of bamboo,
a missionary no longer converting the native gods
into something palatable. Poor you:

Stuck between opium wars and bouts over tea,
your specimens damaged by assistants who didn't care,
the music you hated, the burden of trunks and cases,
your golden monkey skins perishing in the humid air:

Before you return to Tientsin, where the Christians are dead,
ten Daughters of Charity murdered, your mission house blazing,
if only everything could stop at this moment that knows
nothing but the quiet eyes of a new bear, gazing.

Queen of the May

I won't wash my face in the dew at first light:
I never had that maiden skin, rose pink or hawthorn white.
Mine is oil and olive, the dawn water
would run off me like a mother's warning.

I won't heed my grandmother's *piseogs*,
the way she kept the may out of the house
and crossed herself if we came through the door
clutching its starry branches.

No, I'll cross the threshold of summer with a bold stride,
bringing in stars like a promise of harvest.
I'll close my eyes to the shadow of the scythe,
toss my hips at virgins and fairies,
and defy them to deny me
my blooming crown, my sweet bouquet, my *objets trouvés* of
    summer.

I'll heap clusters of flowers on my altar
and be my own Queen of the May,
and I won't believe in anything
except that summer is coming
and May needs nothing else to be magic.

I'll drink wine in the long twilight
with my love in the garden,
lie in the grass and love freckles onto his skin.
I'll dance at his maypole with nothing to lose
but my chains of daisies that each say,
he loves me.

Oh you might as well talk to the wall
(that's crawling with woodbine again)

as lay down the law to me,
feckless and reckless with summer.

Poem for October

October is a greedy month:
Night gobbles at the edges of day;
the forest floor breaks the leaves down
to a dull mulch in the earth's mouth;

the woods hide misers' hordes
and spectres door to door
cross into the other world
as if there were no tomorrow.

October is a prickly time
of beech burs and chestnut spines,
of sweaters that scratch and scarves that itch
your faded summer skin.

Every autumn, I want to burrow down,
muffle up against the chill,
swaddle and hide in a thicker skin
till spring lets the sunshine in.

But today I saw chestnuts fall in the park.
My daughter said they were prickly apples
whispering jokes and bursting with laughter,
the mahogany shining through their slit skirts.

Ah, the chestnuts know how to come out in winter:
They cast themselves into the unknown,
leaping from trees onto crispy leaves,
shedding their thick green dresses.

While humans huddle, the chestnut is saying,
look at me, polished for the autumn!

Tie me to a string and I'll swing all around me.
I am not afraid of any season: I contain a whole world.

Next autumn I'll be a green leaper,
throwing off my thick skin and fighting my corner,
shining a brown light into the winter,
knowing I'm big as a tree inside.

Three Poems for Harry

1. A WORD FOR LOVE

I want to roll you around on my tongue
like a fabulous word,
something with a hint of Italian swagger
for your Neapolitan blood:
Caravaggio, braggadocio, imbroglio;
something muscular and supple,
hard with a soft centre or vice versa:
lascivious, basilica, scintillating;
a phrase to make me drunk and sluttish:
my *uisce beatha*, my lilac wine, my *coteaux de layon*,
then tremble on the edge of sobriety:
my honeysuckle, my hot posset, my dark chocolate.
I want to roll you around on my tongue
like a phonetic alphabet:
my bilabial fricative, my uvular lateral, my plosive,
my glottal
stop.

II. THE SILK ROAD

We come together here to speak the vow
our eyes first made, above the lily-pond
where two reflections shimmered into one,
outside the sunny Silk Road restaurant.

The road beneath our feet is grass and stone.
Its length of seven years behind us charts
our silk route, ribboning from Kimmage West,
its trade, the secrets of our minds and hearts.

And though we don't know where this road may weave,
over what fells and edges it might travel,
we know our home is in each other's arms,
our two yarns spun together can't unravel.

Two perfect equals, plying a fair trade,
exchange today the vows our eyes once made.

III. WAKING AT TARA COVE

Light trembles on lashes. Your eyes
stir deep pools of morning
where I might float or drown.
Your body dawns on me,
our mouths dock and anchor
where the earth ends and the sea begins,
where the sea ends and the earth begins.
We reclaim each other,
snatching a space from the time that rushes in,
as though this moment of skin on flesh on skin

could absolve the blanked out, the blackouts,
the sodden sheets, the drunken bouts,
the one-night stands, the one-stand nights,
the cracks in your heart, the rips in my tights.

Holding you now against all we've weighed and wanted
and feeling love tilt the balance on our side:
We're still looking into each other's surprised eyes
and casting off, with a blessing instead of a curse,
the ones that should have been better,
the ones that could have been worse.

Reines Claudes Dorées

We came to Beaugas in the heatwave
to harvest your greengages
and found the *Reines Claudes Dorées,*
a queen's ransom in the trees.

I felt myself full of promise,
a life three weeks inside me,
so new I told you only
to turn away your *eau de vie.*

On the orchard grass, bittersweet windfalls
blown down before their time.
It had happened twice before,
but this time I felt fruitful, sure.

Between mornings and afternoons of picking golden fruit,
leaping for high branches,
stripping them almost bare,
we rested in the shade at noon.

I sat warm on a fallen tree
with my love, my friend, my friend's love, and my child-to-be,
with plums like sunshine bursting in my mouth
and thought, *this is enough.*

Sometimes the fruit was sticky:
Insects had got there first,
their entrance marked by
a thin trickle of honey.

And, though overnight we kept the plums
cool as the baking dark allowed,
their bloom had lost a shade by morning
for their trip to *la coopérative.*

Queen Claude would be forgotten
except for these small fruits:
Her years a bare two dozen,
her back bent almost double,
her memory is made perfect by
these gold globes streaked with green,
misty like opals,
luscious.

In the gloom of our summer,
I think of your orchard
where for a week we panned for gold
in rivers of *Reines Claudes* trees.

With nuggets big as walnuts
we packed the wooden boxes,
our arms and mouths and bellies
so full,
            so full,
                        so full.

Transformer

You crashland on the planet,
sleeping till a quake rips a ravine
across the world, the old wounds erupting,
unearthing the ghost in the machine.

A robot shifting to a rocket ship,
simple enough to blast imagination.
Small fingers, minds earth their magic in you,
hypnotising themselves into a fascination.

Shrinking into yourself, or big enough
to save or scoff the race,
you're more than meets the eye,
a bridge from outer to inner space.

You relish your own language:
Autobot, Decepticon, Vector Sigma,
the earth's fate lisping in your mouth,
little shapeshifter, changeling, enigma.

Scooter

Between our sure steps you pick your way
slowly at first, one foot ticking on the path,
the other planted on your new scooter.

Quickly, unexpectedly,
you stutter into your stride
till you are gliding, feet together,
just ahead.

While we exchange shy smiles of pride
you are suddenly farther on,
heartshockingly small beside the open road,
a skater on cracked ice
where big children knife by on bicycles.

There's a flashback to that first crawl
when the house bulged with dangers:
The fireplace a bludgeon for your head,
the table corner a spike for your eye,
the kitchen a nerve centre of poisons and avalanches.

Now we gasp into a run
at your heedless happiness
as you round the corner,
as we round the corner,
watching the gap widening.

Night Before School

It had rained all day, driving round Inverin and Moycullen,
the landscape smudged like a child's painting,
the road a wet blackboard.

You slept most of the way home to Dublin,
your longest nap since you curled in a sling
just the other side of my womb.

I was the one stir crazy,
knowing what was ahead of you:
Hemmed into a uniform, a small desk and chair,
the compulsory sitting, your ceaseless chatter stifled.

And then the sun blessed us with a last kick of summer,
our small garden golden and glittering with drops,
the apples glowing fairytale red.

We postponed dinner for Poddle Park.
You pedalled an heirloom bike through the slanting light
and I walked behind, drinking you in,
seeing how summer had grown you.

In my shadow, I'm a big girl, you laughed,
and the late sun flung a long figure on a high nelly
stretching away from us
over the shaking grass.

Something Out of Nothing Soup

When you call from France
I say I'm writing about food
and you remind me of the soup I made
in our London bedsit.

While one of us cooked,
the other soaked in the big bath in the kitchen
figuring out new ways to fool
the metre that gobbled our fifty pences.

Working yet another 'back week' in the '80s,
cash poor, dream rich,
we'd shop in Sainsbury's
heaping our trolley with luxuries.

Your favourite was a steeply-priced cheesecake,
the glossy fruit encased in ruby jelly,
the cream cheese impossibly high and white,
the base pale as champagne.

Our mouths watered as you placed it
high at the front of the trolley
where other people put small children.

As we nosed towards the checkout
we took everything out again:
chocolate biscuits, ginger crackers, your father's gourmet relishes,
we replaced on reproachful shelves.

Last of all,
you'd bring the cheesecake carefully back to its fridge
as I crossed the last aisle.
Some day, you'd say.

At the checkout we'd pay for
our bag of flour, our bread and porridge.
We lived on pancakes for a fortnight.
When the eggs ran out, and then the milk,
we made them from flour and water.

And one evening for a change,
I decided to make soup.
There was nothing to make soup with
but I boiled water anyway,
made a stock of salt and pepper
and dried herbs left by a previous tenant.

It was delicious, savoury,
we relished its simplicity.
you said God was not the only one
who could make something out of nothing.

When at last I got paid, I bought the cheesecake for you.
I carried it to the counter like an offertory gift.
It was the day you turned the telly on its side
so you could watch it lying on the sofa.

Side-by-side we bit into
the taste of disappointment:
The cream cheese stuck to the roofs of our mouths,
its fruit artificially sweet, its base soft and sickly.

I'd thought we would treasure the time
we finally ate that cheesecake,
but on the phone from France
your voice is warm with the memory of
Something Out of Nothing Soup.

Sonnet of a Five-String Banjo

An African mother in the Appalachians
gave birth to my flat-bellied incantations.
I'm fingerpickin', real hot lickin',
giddy to the neck like a headless chicken.
I'm a sleight of hand, a one-man band,
a corny, born-again journeyman.
I'm a god, a gourd, a hurdy-gurdy,
I'm a country girl that's plain and purty.
I'm a country boy, Mama's pride and joy,
I'm all wound up like a clockwork toy.
I'm a pequeniño, a pickin' ninny,
a shindig granny, a hootenanny.
I'm a coal miner, a gold miner,
a moonshiner, a lonesome piner.

In a grass of my own, I'm blue and new,
I'm rare old, fair old mountain dew.
I'm a railroad car sliding down the fret,
I'm a runaway freight but I'll run back yet.
I'm a lonesome whistle, hopin' this'll
pierce your heart like a fresh-picked thistle.
I'm a square dancer, a quare dancer,
a bit of a chancer with a smart answer.
I'm a necromancer, a patched pantser,
an old time, gold time rhyme romancer:
I'm a banjo, I'm a banshee,
you can ban everybody but you can't ban me.
(No sirree)
I'm flailin' and wailin' like an old banshee,
You can ban anybody but you
can't   ban   me
(dum-diddley-i-die)
not me!

The Ballad of Síle Na Gig

I

Come gather round, boys, and come gather round, men,
I'll show ye a sight that ye won't see again,
though you may think it little, its impact is big,
come list to my story, I'm Síle na Gig.

II

And what is a gig, did I hear you enquire?
The answer's the apex of all your desire:
a gig is the elegant carriage you see,
right under my belly: my Síle na Gee.

III

Like the gig with two wheels it can give you a ride,
you'll be cosy and cosseted snugly inside,
as a whirligig jiggles you down a green lane,
so your Síle na Gig jolts you nearly in twain.

IV

You'll be hard from Fethard to the Tower at Rattoo,
to Kilsarkan where I have a womb with a view,
to Cashel and Doon, where I lie on my side,
holding open my casket with evident pride.

V

On to Ballynahinch where I'm clicking my heels,
come click with me, darlin', and see how it feels,
it starts like a waltz and it ends like a jig,
the dance that you'll dance with a Síle na Gig.

VI

Some say I remind them that death hurries near,
ye came into the world by the gap ye see here,

and ye'll die a wee death every time ye go in,
but there's life in me still, I'm a decent oul' skin.

VII
Some think I'm a warning put up by a bishop,
to show Adam's race what the devil can dish up.
Like Eve with her apple, I don't give a fig,
I'm a whore to the core, is old Síle na Gig.

VIII
You may hunt high and low for a maidenly kiss,
but to all who come hunting I'll promise them this,
for my womanly treasure they won't have to dig,
it's all out in the open with Síle na Gig.

IX
Call me witch, call me bitch, I'm the true divine hag,
I'm stone but not flagstone for I never flag.
A flasher, a smasher, come pimp or come prig,
I've got it, I flaunt it, says Síle na Gig.

Leonardo's Cradle Song

*It seemed to me that, while I was in my cradle, a kite came to me
and opened my mouth with its tail, and struck me several times
with its tail inside my lips.* (Da Vinci, Notebooks, 1504)

In my cradle I dreamed that a bird touched my lip
and my cradle rose up like a great flying ship.
Feathers shall raise us, as feathers raise birds,
though quills be our feathers, though wings be but words.

In my cradle I dreamed that a bird touched my lip.
I will soar like the swift, like the swallow I'll dip.
Though one without wings will be carried to heaven,
he who sits down with twelve will rise up with eleven.

In my cradle I dreamed that a bird touched my lip
and its claws took me up in their terrible grip.
My friends I have gathered, my table I've laid,
yet truly I say that I shall be betrayed.

In my cradle I dreamed that wings opened my mouth.
With the swallows in winter my soul will fly south.
I have fashioned the feast of the loaf without leaven
and bread without yeast will rise upwards to heaven.

In my cradle I dreamed a great beating of wings.
Though the small bird be caged, ever louder it sings.
As the grape must be pressed so it yields the best wine,
my crushed heart takes wings to become the divine.

Peppers

for Sandy

When I heard you were moving from Paterson,
I worried about the peppers on your deck.
People can take root anywhere
but what about those pale stems weighed with jewels?

Creamy moonstones, amethysts ripening to garnets,
teardrops of green, tiny orange earrings,
globes yellow as a child's sun,
small spheres dark as chocolate:

You fostered nations: Thai Yellow, Chinese Red;
plucked them like flowers: Summer Sweet, Pretty in Purple;
flourished them like Cuban cigars:
Habanero, serrano, jalapeño.

In the dim kitchen they were everywhere:
fruit and vegetable, salad, spice;
warm as welcomes, sweet as sugar,
tearjerkers, mouthfire.

The Caribbean people on your block:
Dominicans, black West Indians,
felt the sun suddenly tropical as they passed,
stopped to marvel at this sudden burst of home.

They lifted their faces to
your deck rich as a marketplace
strung with lanterns or beads,
each plant a festive tree.

Your porch steps drew their homesick feet.
They called to bargain or barter,
and gently, from tender branches,
you picked bagfuls of their memories.

When I heard you were moving from Paterson,
I had a pang for the tang of your capsicums,
I dreamed of the collective name for them:
A heatwave, an astonishment, a perplexity of peppers.

For the moment we eke out the bag of chillies
Dried to slender pods of red
That you poured from a rainbow of jars.
Each one can warm a tableful.

When I heard you were moving from Paterson,
I wished you well in your new home, of course,
But I hope your deck has its own weather
and warm stems bend with jewels on your porch.

Six Scenes with Olives

I
Over my parents' bed, the thick crucifix
was a *memento mori*.
Christ could slide away to reveal
a space for water, beads and a phial
of rich oil, the extreme unction.

II
In the place of the olive press, *Gethsemane*,
he was crushed, the chrism
forced out of his shrivelling skin
and falling as blood
onto the garden.

III
In the lost Caravaggio,
Christ on the Mount of Olives,
he is buckling over two sleeping forms,
while Peter, startled awake,
is Judas in *The Taking of Christ*,
looking fearfully to the future.

IV
No one is poor who has an olive tree,
the old chef tells me.
He is looking back to Palestine,
his eyes black and soft with home.
This tree is the god in our garden.
It is not food alone.
It gives us cures and candles,
leaves to feed our goats,
summer shade and winter wood.
In my country, the olives take us over,

breathe out of our skin and hair
until we are part of each other.

V
As a child,
I was sent to the chemist for a tiny bottle.
It was the myrrh of the medicine cabinet,
warmed drop by drop for ear-ache and cradle-cap,
its scent of somewhere else, warm grass and ease.

VI
Sit opposite me now and we'll anoint our tongues,
dip our bread in unctuous meadowsweet or bitter green,
say a rosary of olive stones.

I won't ask you to stay awake
when the world presses down,
I won't chide your lidded eyes,
your sleeping form is warmth enough.

One day this rite we share
may be extreme.
Till then, my love, I'll bless
our ordinary unction.

Rosemary

The first time we stood in my garden
you admired the rosemary:
holding its hundred arms aloft,
rubbing shoulders with us,
making a charmed circle.

You closed your eyes,
bruised a stem in your hands, took a long breath,
and in the heart of summer I inhaled winter, incense,
all my Christmases.

Where rosemary flourishes, you said, *the woman rules the house*,
and somehow it thrives here under my neglect.
I am grateful for its permanence, glad of its power,
and though I need no ointment, salve or liniment,
I have only to reach my arm to find
a sprig for my pillow to ward off witches,
a tea for headaches, wine for gout, a purseful against plague,
an oil to mummify, a torch to purify,
a spear for friendship, remembrance, love.

My grandmother said rosemary never grew taller than Christ
nor older than his years on earth.
We have two decades yet before we know for sure.

Meanwhile ours is rich and handsome
and we are rosemary spendthrifts,
turning shoulders and legs of lamb into porcupines
with forests of fragrant spines,
studding the roast pork,
sprinkling the salads,
spiking the summer potatoes,
stirring it through Italian sauces.

In summer, when our daughter is asleep,
the garden calls us out.
We drink in the last of the light
and breathe the incense inching up the wall.
Brighter greens come and go, but always
it is dark green above, downy grey under,
and suddenly a scatter of lilac stars.

ACKNOWLEDGEMENTS

Acknowledgements are due to the editors of the following publications in which some of these new poems, or versions of them, have been published:

'Naming a Bridge' was published in *Rosie: Essays in Honour of Rosanna 'Rosie' Hackett (1893–1976): Revolutionary and Trade Unionist,* edited by Mary McAuliffe (Arlen House, 2015);

'The Dark Room' and 'Daughter' were published in *The Level Crossing* (Dedalus Press, 2016);

'The Shoe Box Coffin' was runner-up in the Francis Ledwidge International Poetry Award 2014. 'Pocket Knife' was shortlisted in 2015;

'The Rebel Sisterhood' was commissioned by BeRnzy Mac for Eastrogen Rising: A Rebel Cabaret, and first performed at the Five Lamps Arts Festival, Dublin in March 2016;

'The Man Who Was Not a Baker' was commissioned by Rang a Trí, Scoil Naithí, Ballinteer, during a residency in Autumn 2015;

'The One Who Shoots Stones' was written for Palestinian Culture Night 2015 at The New Theatre, Dublin.

Many thanks to Noel King, editor, Doghouse Books for publishing the two collections, *A Bone in My Throat* (2007) and *Strange Familiar* (2013), from which the other poems in this volume are drawn. The poems 'Meeting at the Chester Beatty' and 'Grange Abbey, Donaghmede' were included in *If Ever You Go: A Map of Dublin in Poetry and Song,* edited by Pat Boran and Gerard Smyth (Dedalus Press, 2014).

Thanks to Felim Egan for facilitating the use of the cover image from the Windows into Gaza exhibition he curated in 2014; do Professor Margaret Kelleher, 'fairy godmother' agus comharsan béal dorais; agus do Harry, mo chéadsearc.

Thanks to my mother, Mary – a topper; and to Pat Boran for conceiving and patiently nurturing this book.